The Camping Trip

By Marcie Aboff
Illustrated by Solana Pagan

Scott Foresman
is an imprint of

Glenview, Illinois • Boston, Massachusetts • Chandler, Arizona •
Upper Saddle River, New Jersey

Photographs

Every effort has been made to secure permission and provide appropriate credit for photographic material. The publisher deeply regrets any omission and pledges to correct errors called to its attention in subsequent editions.

Unless otherwise acknowledged, all photographs are the property of Pearson Education, Inc.

12 Stephen Oliver/©DK Images.

ISBN 13: 978-0-328-50846-4
ISBN 10:   0-328-50846-2

14 15 V010 18 17 16 15

Josh, Mom, and Dad were packing for a camping trip. They went camping every year.

Josh loved camping, but this year wasn't the same. His older brother Troy was away at college.

Josh missed his brother. Troy had helped Josh with soccer, with computer games, and with homework. And Troy always led the way on the hiking trails.

Before Troy left, he patted Josh on the back.

"You're in charge now, buddy," he said.

Josh and his parents drove up the mountains. They traveled past many tall trees. The winding road led them to their campsite.

"It's as perfect as I remember it," said Mom.

The campsite was in a clearing near a small pond. A large lake was on the other side of the pond.

"Let's go swimming," Josh said.

"We must set up camp first," said Dad.

Josh helped Mom and Dad set up the tent. Nearby, he could hear the water as it crashed down a cliff, spilling into the lake. He remembered swimming in the lake and splashing Troy with water.

Later in the afternoon, Josh and his parents walked to the stable to see the horses.

Josh got on a horse and sat in the saddle. He was able to gallop with his horse this year.

"Great job, Josh!" Mom said.

"You've really come a long way," said Dad.

After their ride, Josh and his parents walked back to their tent.

"Tomorrow we'll go hiking," said Dad.

Josh remembered their hike last year. Troy had led it. He knew about all the plants and animals they saw.

That night Josh helped Mom and Dad build a fire. The weather turned cool, so Josh put on his jacket. He felt something in the pocket. He took it out. It was a compass.

Josh smiled. Troy had given Josh his compass before he left for college.

Josh turned the compass. The arrow inside moved. When Josh held the compass, Troy didn't seem so far away.

"Hey, Dad," Josh said. "I have something for our hike tomorrow." He held up the compass. "This year, I'll lead the way!"

A Compass

A compass is a tool that tells direction. It helps people get from one place to another. A compass is used by campers, drivers, pilots, mariners, and hunters.

The compass can help us find directions—north, south, east, and west. A compass has a magnetic needle for a pointer. The compass magnet follows the magnetic force of the earth's north and south poles.